Basil Brush and the Windmills

by

Peter Firmin

Prentice-Hall, Inc., Englewood Cliffs, New Jersey

Copyright © 1979 by Kaye & Ward Ltd.

First American edition published 1980 by Prentice-Hall, Inc.,
Englewood Cliffs, N.J.

Printed in the United States of America   •J
Prentice-Hall International, Inc., London
Prentice-Hall of Australia, Pty. Ltd., North Sydney
Prentice-Hall of Canada, Ltd., Toronto
Prentice-Hall of India Private Ltd., New Delhi
Prentice-Hall of Japan, Inc., Tokyo
Prentice-Hall of Southeast Asia Pte. Ltd., Singapore
Whitehall Books Limited, Wellington, New Zealand
              1 2 3 4 5 6 7 8 9 10

Library of Congress Cataloging in Publication Data

Firmin, Peter.
  Basil Brush and the windmills.

    SUMMARY: With only one penny left with which to pay the
electricity, water, and gas bills, Basil Brush and his friend
Harry the mole decide to live like they did in the old days and
build windmills for power.
    [1. Windmills—Fiction. 2. Foxes—Fiction.
3. Moles (Animals)—Fiction] I. Title.
PZ7.F49873Bap 1979   [E]   80-10178
ISBN 0-13-066720-X

Basil Brush and the Windmills

Basil Brush is a fox. He lives in a
house with a mailbox by the gate.
Harry is a mole. He went to the mailbox
to get the mail.

There were letters to read.
There were bills to pay.
"Bills and more bills," groaned Basil.
"Bills for electricity, bills for water
and gas."

Basil opened his money box.
"Look," he said. "All these bills to pay
and only one penny left!"

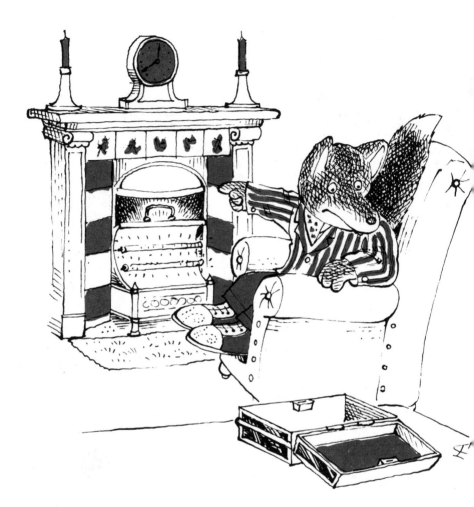

He sat in front of the heater.
"Look at it," he moaned. "Burning our money . . .
I'll wipe the smile off its face."

He switched off the heater.
"But I'm cold," said Harry.
"Well, move about a bit," said Basil.
"Do some work. That's the way to stay warm."

So Harry got out the vacuum cleaner to do some cleaning. He switched it on.
"Look at it," said Basil. "It sucks up the dirt but it eats up our money."

He switched off the cleaner and put it away.
Harry swept up with a broom.

"I'm hungry," said Harry.
He boiled some eggs on the gas stove.
"Look at that," said Basil. "It boils our
eggs but our money goes up in the steam."
He turned off the gas.
"We'll have our eggs soft," he said.

12

"Oh," said Harry. "You are being hard."
"Well it costs too much," said Basil.
"But we must eat," said Harry.
"We have to keep warm."

"People did not need gas and electricity
long ago," said Basil, " and they kept warm.
We'll live like they did in the old days.
We'll have a real fire. We'll burn wood."
"You mean like they did in the merry evil
days?" said Harry.

"Exactly," said Basil. "I'll clear out the
fireplace while you fetch the wood."
So Basil took out the heater.
He opened up the fireplace and lit a fire.

They boiled a kettle and made some tea.
They fried some eggs and made toast.
"I'm bored," said Harry. "Can I have
the television on?"

"Oh, no," said Basil. "People did not have
television in the old days. We'll entertain
ourselves. We'll make our own television."
Basil put a large picture frame on some
chairs and draped a curtain over it.

"Hello, folks!" called Basil through the
frame. "This is your own . . . your favorite . . .
the one and only singing and joking fox . . .
Basil Brush — Boom Boom!
Now you have to clap."
Harry clapped politely.

Basil went on:
"I say I say I say, which side of a cup
is the handle? . . . Give up? Then I'll
tell you. The outside.
That's where you laugh."
"Ha ha! Hee hee hee!" laughed Harry. "You're
very good. Just like the real thing."

"Now fans . . . it's request time," Basil
went on. "For little Harry of Tooting, a song—
    Harreeee . . . Harreeeeeeeeeee . . .
    Pride of our Alleeeeeee . . ."

Harry walked up to the curtains and
carefully pulled them over the frame.
"I don't like this TV show," he said.
"I've turned you into a radio,
so that I can hear the news."

"I'll give you the news," hissed Basil.
"Here is the news, and this is Basil
Brush reading it. Today, Basil, a
well-known fox, punched his best friend,
Harry, a mole, on the nose!"
"That didn't happen," said Harry.

"It will if you aren't careful," said Basil.
"I am doing my best to amuse you and you are
not a bit grateful!"
"Well, I'm bored," said Harry. "What can I do?"
"Oh, amuse yourself," said Basil.
"Make something. Make a toy."

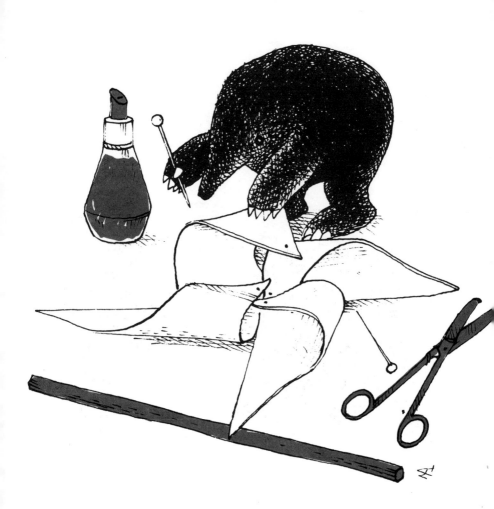

Harry took some paper and wood.
He made a paper windmill.
He stuck it in the window box.
The wind made it spin.

Basil looked at the windmill spinning.
"There is power in the wind," he said.
"I will make a big windmill to work the
saw. It will cut wood for the fire."

Basil took wood and pieces of cloth.
He took wheels and bits of wire.
He soon built a windmill.
He fixed a saw to it and used
the garden seat as a saw horse.
He put a log of wood in place
and climbed up to the sails.

"Stand back!" he called.
"I'm starting it now."
The wind blew.
The sails turned.
The wheels spun.

The saw slid back and forth cutting the wood.

"It works!" said Basil.
The log was soon cut but the saw did not
stop. It cut right through the garden seat.
It buried itself in the ground and broke.
But the windmill did not stop.

Basil jumped down.
"Well, let it turn," he said.
"It's doing no harm."
Harry looked at the pieces of garden seat.
"That should burn well," he said.

They carried the wood indoors and
put it on the fire. Harry made the
fire burn with a pair of bellows.
"The wind has blown sawdust into the
house," he said. "It's made a terrible mess.
Can I clean it up with the vacuum cleaner?"

"Oh, no," said Basil. "They did not have
vacuum cleaners in the old days."
He looked at the bellows.
"If I made another windmill," he said,
"it would work some large bellows,
we could use it as a vacuum cleaner."

Basil took more wood and things.
He soon built another windmill.
He made a large pair of bellows with canvas.
He led a hose into the house.

"Ready!" he called. "I'm starting it now."
The wind blew.
The sails turned.
The wheels spun.
The bellows puffed in and out.
"It works!" shouted Basil.

The bellows did work, but they did not suck.
They blew.
They blew air down the hose and blew
soot and sawdust all over the house.

Harry tried to hold the hose but it
twisted and turned like an angry snake
and blew him out of the door.

"Turn it off!" he shouted to Basil.
"Don't be silly," said Basil. "I can't
turn off the wind!"
Harry dragged the hose out of the house.

"I'm hot and I'm tired," he said. "I'm
covered in dust. I need a cold bath."
"You can use the water in the well," said
Basil. "A windmill would pull it up."

Basil made another windmill. He fixed it
to a long lever. It lifted buckets of cold water
from the well and tipped them over Harry.

"Enough," called Harry. "Stop it now."
Basil could not stop it. It lifted more
and more water from the well.
Harry was clean but very cold and wet.

"I'd like to get dry now," said Harry.
"May I use the hair dryer?"
"Oh, no," said Basil. "But I could make . . ."
"No, thanks," said Harry. "I'd rather run
about to get dry."

Harry ran around and around the garden.
He saw people looking over the fence.
They were looking at the windmills.
Harry ran indoors and got Basil's money box.
He opened the gate.

"Come on! Come on!" he shouted. "See
how we solve our energy problems. See Basil
Brush and his Wonderful Windmills!
Only fifty cents. Come on! Come on!"

The people put money in the money box.
They walked around the garden.
"Ingenious," they cried.
"Wonderful," they sighed.

"What do you mean?" asked Basil. "How *do* we
solve our energy problems?"
Harry showed Basil the money in the box.
"We can pay our bills now," he said.
"Run in and turn on the electric fire,
my friend."